IMAGES
of America

CAMP ROBINSON
AND THE MILITARY
ON THE NORTH SHORE

The 35th Division of the United States Army had been in training at Camp Robinson for most of the year when the Japanese attacked Pearl Harbor on December 7, 1941. The division was soon boarding trains bound for defense duty on the West Coast and would later play a major role in the fighting in Europe. The photograph above symbolized a frequent sight at training posts around the nation in times of war; the training was finished, and the time to go to war at hand, be it by ship, by train, or by air. (NARA.)

ON THE COVER: The young soldiers of Camp Pike were captured washing their dishes in 1917 outside their barracks. (NARA.)

IMAGES
of America

CAMP ROBINSON AND THE MILITARY ON THE NORTH SHORE

Ray Hanley on behalf of the
MacArthur Museum of Arkansas Military History

ARCADIA
PUBLISHING

Published by Arcadia Publishing
Charleston, South Carolina

Printed in the United States of America

Library of Congress Control Number: 2013945319

For all general information, please contact Arcadia Publishing:
Telephone 843-853-2070
Fax 843-853-0044
E-mail sales@arcadiapublishing.com
For customer service and orders:
Toll-Free 1-888-313-2665

Visit us on the Internet at www.arcadiapublishing.com

*This book is dedicated to the hundreds of thousands of men and
women who came to the north shore of the Arkansas River from
all parts of the nation and from all walks of life to train their minds
and bodies in the service of the United States of America.*

CONTENTS

FOREWORD

In the late 1880s, the US War Department decided to close hundreds of small arsenals it operated throughout the country and establish a few large military posts near railroad centers to facilitate quick deployment of troops. The immediate effect of this 19th-century version of BRAC (base realignment and closure) was the end of the Little Rock Arsenal, which had functioned as a military post since 1840. The arsenal had witnessed pivotal exchanges during the Civil War and would one day become famous as the birthplace of General of the Army Douglas MacArthur. On April 23, 1892, the federal government transferred the buildings and grounds to the city of Little Rock with the provision that the grounds would be "forever exclusively devoted to the uses and purposes of a public park for said City." Little Rock lost its first arsenal but gained its first public park.

The closure of the Little Rock Arsenal paved the way for a larger military presence across the Arkansas River, which endures to this day. As word reached Little Rock that the arsenal grounds must be abandoned, local, state, and congressional leaders negotiated a deal whereby the federal government traded the 36-acre site in return for 1,000 acres of privately owned property on Big Rock Mountain, in what is now North Little Rock. Pres. William McKinley declared the new site would be named Fort Roots in 1897 in honor of Logan H. Roots, a prominent Little Rock businessman who was instrumental in securing both the city park and the new military post and who had died four years earlier.

Fort Roots trained troops until World War I, when officials realized it was not sufficient for the needs of a growing military. The War Department selected a larger Argenta (today's North Little Rock) site with easier access, and Camp Pike opened in 1917, quickly replacing Fort Roots as a major training facility. The former site maintained a hospital for soldiers during the 1918 influenza epidemic and continues to serve as a veterans' hospital today, with many of the post's original buildings still in use. Arkansas native Maj. John Fordyce oversaw construction of Camp Pike, which was completed in less than six months using 10,000 workers. After the war ended, another land trade occurred. This time, the United Stated deeded 6,500 acres of land to Arkansas with two provisions: the site would be used primarily for military purposes and the federal government could reclaim the property in the event of an emergency.

Between the two world wars, Camp Pike became headquarters for the Arkansas National Guard as well as a large Civilian Conservation Corps unit. In 1937, it was renamed Camp Robinson in honor of the late Joseph T. Robinson, a US senator from Arkansas. By early 1940, the United States exercised its right to reclaim the post and gave it a new role as a replacement training center during World War II. Camp Robinson grew to more than 32,000 acres and became Arkansas's second-largest city, with an average daily population of 50,000. By the time training ended in 1946 and the land reverted back to the State of Arkansas, more than 750,000 soldiers had been trained there.

Over the years, portions of Camp Robinson have been given to other organizations for military use, including reserve centers for Arkansas's Army, Navy and Marine Corps, as well as for use as a veterans' cemetery. Today, it continues to serve as home for the Arkansas National Guard's Joint Forces Headquarters and other Arkansas National Guard units. From its origins on a small 36-acre site on the outskirts of Little Rock to a much larger and sustained presence north of the river, the military in central Arkansas has a rich heritage of service, sacrifice, and honor.

—Stephen McAteer, Executive Director
MacArthur Museum of Arkansas Military HIstory

ACKNOWLEDGMENTS

This book on the military history of the north shore of the Arkansas River has come together with the essential help of a number of people who helped with photographs and the stories behind the photographs. I would like to thank first and foremost Steve Rucker, who runs the Arkansas National Guard Museum (ANGM) on modern-day Camp Robinson, one of the finest in the nation; his help with World War II–era photographs was vital. Chaplain Jackie Ryan at Fort Roots Hospital was quick to help with information for chapter one. Stephen McAteer, who directs the McArthur Museum of Arkansas Military History, was supportive, as was Brian Robertson at the Butler Center for Arkansas Studies. Gratitude goes to Tracy Nieser for the excellent research he did in 1986 for the Pulaski County Historical Review, upon which I drew information. Thanks go to Arcadia Publishing for sharing my vision to turn this tribute to the soldiers who dedicated themselves to service into this book. Photograph credits include John Fordyce of Little Rock for the construction photos in chapter two; other photograph credits in the captions are as follows: National Archives Records Administration (NARA), John Fordyce (JF), and Butler Center for Arkansas Studies (BCAS). All other images appear courtesy of the author's collection.

The jeep came into its own for the Army during World War II, but it was not designed for the use it was put to at Camp Robinson on this day in November 1943. Capt C.R. Goodwin, projects officer with the 66th Division, was seated in the jeep, likely not knowing if he was going forward or backward with his vehicle being used in place of the traditional training sled. (NARA.)

Raymond Palls, left, and Robert Hawthorne were but two of the thousands of young men who were drafted, or enlisted, to serve in the US Army during World War I. They very likely had only recently been issued their uniforms and went to Ewing photography studio near the Camp Pike train depot to have their picture made and put onto postcards to mail home.

INTRODUCTION

Arkansas, from its pre-statehood pioneer days, has always been among the quickest to answer the nation's call in times of war. Cemeteries across the state hold the remains of dozens of men who fought in the Revolutionary War to grant the new nation its freedom. Most moved to Arkansas after the war, like the notable Maj. Henry Francis, hero of the Battle of King's Mountain in South Carolina. He died in 1840 and rests in a Johnson County Cemetery.

A visit to the Arkansas State Capitol lawn finds more evidence of the patriotism of Arkansas at the monument to the statesmen awarded the Congressional Medal of Honor from the Indian wars of the west, the Civil War, World War I, World War II, Korea, and Vietnam.

As remarkable as the record of Arkansas veterans that answered the call to battle is, so too is the role a few thousand acres of land on the north shore of the Arkansas River across from Little Rock played in training countless soldiers for combat.

The first military installation on the north shore was Fort Logan H. Roots, which rose atop a landmark cliff often just called Big Rock. The Mountain Park resort hotel opened on the site in 1887 where only a vineyard had been earlier. The view was described as "the grandest in the state" in June 1887 in the *Arkansas Gazette*. Soon after, the top of the cliff became known as Mountain Park, visited by many local citizens who believed it was at least five degrees cooler than the city of Little Rock, which was sprawled across the river. The popular park would be sacrificed in 1893 to meet the country's military needs and, not insignificantly, boost the area's economy.

At the time, the area known today as North Little Rock was the sixth ward of the city of Little Rock. Mayor H.L. Fletcher and Congressman W.L. Terry—along with other civic and business leaders, such as Logan Roots, a Union army officer who marched with General Sherman and for whom the fort would be named—struck a deal to trade the mountaintop to the secretary of war in exchange for getting the Little Rock Arsenal Grounds on Ninth Street. The city got a new park much closer to most of its citizens, and the US Army got a commanding mountaintop upon which to build a new fort. The military was already in the process of closing smaller military facilities around the country, including the Little Rock Arsenal. In the swap, Little Rock got one of the much-coveted new posts that would bring many soldiers and a significant amount of money for the local economy.

Before 1921, Fort Roots was decommissioned as an Army post and given to the US Public Health Service. By then, a new, even larger military presence had risen a few miles away in 1917. Local business leaders raised $500,000, purchased 3,000 acres, and leased another 10,000 acres northeast of Argenta (today North Little Rock). The land was donated and leased to the US Army for the purpose of building an Army training post as the clouds of war in Europe drifted closer to the United States. The base became the home of the 87th Division and had an official capacity to train just over 43,000 men from Arkansas and surrounding southern states. The base was named Camp Pike after explorer Zebulon Pike.

In 1922, the war having ended some four years earlier and with peace on the horizon, the United States deeded over to Arkansas some 6,500 acres of the former post with the provision that it be used primarily for military activities and that if ever needed, the US government could reclaim it. It was thus that the former Camp Pike became the headquarters of the Arkansas National Guard.

Shortly before World War II, the base was renamed Camp Joseph T. Robinson after the states late senator and governor. Camp Robinson would grow to 32,000 acres during the war and train an estimated 750,000 soldiers by the time training ended in 1946. With an average daily population of some 50,000, Camp Robinson had the second-largest population in the state (if compared to a city).

After the war, portions of the sprawling camp were given to organizations like the Arkansas Game & Fish Commission, while one portion was given to North Little Rock to be used for an airport. A vital part of the land would remain proudly Camp Joseph T. Robinson, which continues even today to train National Guardsmen who remain ready to serve when called to duty by their state or nation.

The end of hard training eventually came for the young soldiers of Camp Pike. They found themselves preparing to ship out for duty, usually by train, with the knowledge that the battlefields of France might be in their future in the weeks and months to come. This young man visited a photographer near the post to have a farewell postcard made.

One

FORT LOGAN H. ROOTS

"Ft. Roots up here," the arrow pointed to the top of Big Rock in this 1907 postcard message. Civic leaders had raised the money and traded a public park atop the mountain to pool some 1,100 acres to entice the US Army to build Fort Logan H. Roots. The business and civic leaders counted on the construction of the facility and its revenue once opened to boost the Greater Little Rock economy.

Arsenal Pike, Driveway to Fort Logan H. Roots,
Little Rock, Ark.

The road to the top of the lofty mountain, where Fort Roots was built, was steep and crooked enough to warrant this 1909 postcard of the road. During construction in the 1890s, wagons hauled all the building materials up these roads from Argenta and Little Rock. The road today is paved, but it retains the same "S" curve.

Near the top of Big Rock, a motorist, or driver of a wagon more likely, would have rolled under this US Military Reservation sign, seen here around 1915.

Among the key civic leaders who had raised the funds and lobbied the US War Department to bring Fort Roots to the top of Big Rock mountain was Logan H. Roots. As a Union army officer, Roots had run General Sherman's supply lines for the thousands of troops that marched across Georgia to the sea. Sadly, Roots did not live to see the completion of the fort that would bear his name, dying suddenly in 1893. His grave, seen here in Oaklawn Cemetery in Little Rock, bears the inscription, "A servant unto the Lord, faithful unto death."

The view from the site of Fort Roots was described as the grandest in the state, and indeed no site had a better view of Little Rock, the capitol of Arkansas, than Big Rock Mountain. The view here looked southeast, back up the Arkansas River, the church steeples and few tall buildings of the city framed by trees. The view today is just as spectacular.

Fort Roots, seen here on a 1908 postcard, was catering to an army in a cavalry era when laid out in the 1890s, hence the large parade ground around which buildings were grouped.

By 1917, the United States' entrance into World War I was on the horizon. The Fort Roots parade group was seeing many automobiles on its encircling driveway. The postcard was written by a soldier in training; he penned, "How is the crop, write me & tell me the news. Am getting as hard as nails, Geo Wildes, 1st troop, 12th reg, Fort Logan H Root, Ark."

Fort Root, Little Rock, Ark.   *Aug. 5, '07.*

Made in Germany. The Dollar Store, C. G. Townsley & Co., Importers, Little Rock, Ark. 316.   Harris, Photographer

Congress set aside $194,760 in 1894 for construction of the first phase of Fort Roots; more money would come later. Successful bidders were given 12 months to finish the buildings, and a 44-gun salute in December 1894 signaled the start of the work. One of the first to be completed was the 45,000-square-foot, 135-man barracks building, erected at a cost of $22,500. "Came here from Fort Sam Houston," wrote a soldier who mailed the card.

Today, the former barracks building is still in service after almost 120 years, though not as a barracks but for other uses by the Fort Roots VA Medical Center. The barracks, along with a number of other late-1800s buildings, have been restored and are in the National Register of Historic Places.

Officer's Row, Fort Logan H Roots, on Big Rock, Argenta, Ark.

Among the first buildings to rise as Fort Roots was constructed was a row of officers' quarters that sat along a curvy lane shaded by large oak trees. The one at the center of this 1911 postcard was built in 1896 at a cost of $14,000 for the 13,000-square-foot house. The row of tree-shaded houses still stands today.

The building above was erected in 1905, designated to serve as a combined post exchange (commissary or store) and gymnasium. "I clerk in this place," wrote a soldier assigned to duty in the commissary in a postcard he mailed home. The building still stands today. (Courtesy of the Butler Center for Arkansas Studies.)

The expanse of the Barracks Building No. 1 is seen well in this frontal-view postcard mailed in 1910. On it was written, "Quarters of Co's A & D, 16th Infantry." The long sprawling building, well maintained, is still in use today; it originally opened in 1896.

At a cost of $26,888, the 28,000-square-foot barracks was built in 1908 to house 65 soldiers. This postcard was mailed in 1910 by H.C McCormick, Co. I, 4th US Infantry. He penciled in the following: "Tom Thumb's wedding at church." The historic building still serves Fort Roots Medical Center today.

With hundreds of young soldiers training atop the mountain, injuries and illnesses were a fact of life. The Fort Roots base hospital, still used today but as offices, was completed in 1896 at a cost of almost $14,000, initially having only 12 beds. The two-story redbrick building originally had wraparound porches gracing both floors, affording patients access to fresh air and sunshine in an era before air-conditioning.

The 9th Infantry Company posed on the porch of one of the Fort Roots barracks around 1916, likely shortly before they shipped out for duty on the Mexican border. Of note is the size of the soldier in the center of the first row.

Bachelor officers fared better at Fort Roots when it came to housing versus the barracks built for enlisted men. The Bachelor Officers' Quarters was completed in 1907, totaling more than 32,000 square feet and costing approximately $32,000. Seen below is the officers' quarters building that has been substantially altered over the years; it still serves as a part of the Fort Roots Medical Center today.

In 1911, the US Army troops stationed at Fort Roots were called upon to assist the veterans of another army who had fought a war 50 years earlier. When Little Rock hosted the annual meeting of the United Confederate Veterans, their promise to house and feed the old soldiers was strained when some 12,000 veterans poured into the city. The commander at Fort Roots dispatched his soldiers with wagons bearing 1,300 canvas tents and erected a vast encampment in Little Rock's City Park. Little Rock kept its commitment to the last of the Confederate army.

The call to defend the nation came to Fort Roots in the weeks after Mexican revolutionary Pancho Viva raided Columbus, New Mexico, in 1916. Twenty-four companies of the Arkansas National Guard were soon in training at Fort Roots and, along with four companies of the 9th Infantry already stationed there, were soon on the Texas-Mexico border. Posed here with guns at the ready, the Arkansas soldiers never crossed the border and saw no combat in General Pershing's unsuccessful mission to run down Viva.

Company D of the 16th Infantry, seen here around 1910, was also based at Fort Roots. The soldiers were dressed in their finest uniform for a formal ceremony, the nature of which is lost in time.

The pace of life at Fort Roots changed markedly when the United States declared war on Germany in April 1917. The country was divided into areas to organize an army, with Arkansas, Louisiana, and Mississippi making up the 12th Divisional Area. The formerly sleepy Fort Roots was transformed into a base for training officers for the activated reserves in the 12th Regiment. Construction of new housing was soon under way, as seen in the reserve camp above.

Written on the back of this June 1917 postcard is the following: "All buildings look alike to me, getting in at 1 AM." A solider named William made note of the long row of seemingly identical wooden barracks, down to the screen doors lined up along a fresh dirt road.

"Making their beds" was the caption on this postcard showing newly arrived troops not even in uniform yet as they took charge of their issued bedding before moving into their raw, new barracks. The young men would train hard, beginning at 6:00 a.m. daily and often not ending until taps at 10:00 p.m. A newly enlisted Army private in 1917 earned $30 a month.

The cliff at the edge of Fort Roots, with its commanding view of the Little Rock and the Arkansas River far below, was a popular backdrop for photographs of young soldiers, such as this one in 1917. As he stared into the camera, perhaps he was thinking of home, or perhaps of the war raging in France for which he might well be bound upon completion of his training. The view for young soldiers on the north shore would soon change, as Fort Roots was too small to meet the growing needs of the Army.

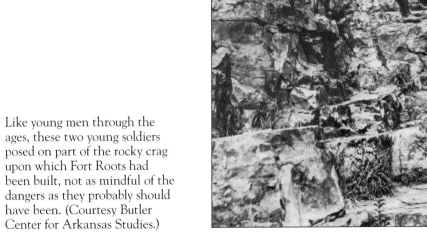

Like young men through the ages, these two young soldiers posed on part of the rocky crag upon which Fort Roots had been built, not as mindful of the dangers as they probably should have been. (Courtesy Butler Center for Arkansas Studies.)

—OLD GLORY—
FORT. LOGAN H.ROOTS. ARK.

Around 1910, Fort Root's hospital building was photographed from out on the post's parade ground, Old Glory flying in a steep breeze. The vast parade ground first laid out when the US Army was in the horse cavalry era remains today, spread out before the historic buildings with a proud flag still present.

V. A. HOSPITAL
NORTH LITTLE ROCK ARKANSAS

Following World War I, Fort Roots was turned over to the US Public Health Service, charged with treating seriously wounded veterans from the conflict. In 1921, under an act sponsored by US senator Joe T. Robinson, Fort Roots was established as a veterans' hospital. The hospital service began in the old prewar barracks buildings; new structures were added over the years, some seen in this c. 1940 aerial view. The Fort Roots VA Hospital, with some 80 buildings, continues today to care for men and women who have served their nation.

Two

CAMP PIKE

"*Our Country! In her intercourse with foreign nations may she always be in the right; but our country, right or wrong.*"
— *Stephen Decatur.*

The Great War, in later years called World War I, began in 1914 with the assassination of the heir to the Austro-Hungarian throne, Archduke Francis Ferdinand, in Sarajevo. The United States resisted involvement for the first three years but finally declared war on Germany on Good Friday, April 6, 1917. A military draft was quickly instituted, and 32 cantonments were planned to train as many as 50,000 men each. The Little Rock Board of Commerce, with private businessmen putting up $300,000, bought several thousand acres of land north of Argenta (today North Little Rock) and convinced the Army to locate one of the sprawling posts on the north shore of the Arkansas River. The new post was named Camp Pike, after early American explorer Zebulon Pike. This postcard, sold at Camp Pike in 1917, shows Pres. Woodrow Wilson and Gen. John J. Pershing expressing the patriotic mood that swept the nation. Most photographs in this chapter are courtesy of John R. Fordyce (JF) of Little Rock, grandson of Maj. John Fordyce, who oversaw the construction of Camp Pike and who had the photographs made.

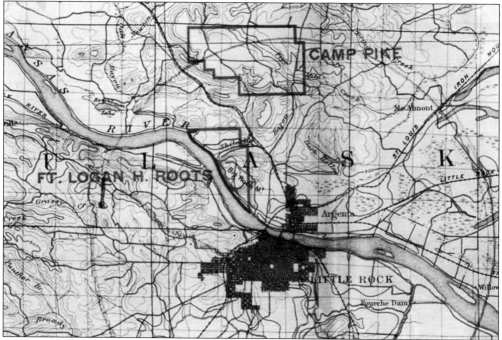

The 1918 topographical map was marked to show the location of Fort Roots and the much larger Camp Pike a few miles to the north and west. What is today North Little Rock is reflected as the small city of Argenta on the map.

In June 1917, the US War Department announced it would spend $3.5 million to build Camp Pike. Over the next three years, the project would bring a monthly payroll to the Greater Little Rock area estimated at $2.5 million. Still, the construction would be daunting and was expected to move at a pace never before seen in Arkansas. The first roads were laid out into the sprawling rural countryside with the aide of surveyors, like this crew standing in the middle of a freshly graded dirt path. (ANGM.)

Training the replacement soldiers the Army expected to need in Europe could not await the construction of barracks, and the first group of draftees and those enlisting were housed in long rows of tents as construction got under way on a more permanent post.

EARLY DAYS, CAMP PIKE, LITTLE ROCK, ARK.

The job of overseeing the construction of Camp Pike was assigned to Maj. John R. Fordyce. Born in Alabama in 1869, young Fordyce moved to Hot Springs, Arkansas, in the 1870s, where his wealthy father became a major figure. After graduating as an engineer from Washington University, Fordyce invented machinery for processing cotton. The successful engineer was commissioned as a major in the Engineers Reserve Corps of the US Army in April 1917. He was there for the start of the construction for the first building of Camp Pike on June 26, 1917. (JF.)

Housing and facilities to train up to 40,000 men required a construction effort unlike anything seen before in Arkansas. Before the completion of a railroad spur into the camp, men and materials moved from the rail depots in nearby Argenta and Little Rock by wagon trains, one of which is seen here as mules pull it. (JF.)

The age of the cavalry that had reigned when nearby Fort Roots opened in the 1890s had given way to a much more mechanized Army by World War I. Still, the machinery that poured in to help build Camp Pike was not fail-safe. Above, a team of mules is being used to pull a truck at the construction site. (JF.)

Horses and mules were an essential part of the workforce while building Camp Pike. The auxiliary remount depot at the post took care of almost 4,000 horses and mules assigned to the operations. Remount Road, a familiar route name even today, took its name from the original road into the camp's remount depot. (JF.)

The thousands of acres of land that the Army accumulated to build Camp Pike had seen pioneer settlers in the 1800s; one family of settlers left behind this log cabin with its wooden shake shingles. (JF.)

The workforce recruited to build Camp Pike was, at its peak, around 10,000 men. They ranged from manual labor—like the ones seen here building a road—to skilled carpenters, electricians, and plumbers. (JF.)

Lines formed at the end of each week as the civilian laborers eagerly awaited their pay. The workers' payroll averaged a reported $300,000 a week, a huge boost to the area's economy. (JF.)

Maj. John Fordyce, in command of building Camp Pike, quickly worked with the Missouri & Iron Mountain Railroad to bring a spur line from Argenta into the emerging Army post. This greatly improved the ability to move into Fort Pike the vast amount of building materials needed, such as the lumber being unloaded above. (JF.)

Loading docks and huge warehouses soon took shape to receive the equipment and supplies pouring daily into the rapidly rising Camp Pike. (JF.)

One arrival by a railroad flatcar that greatly helped pick up the pace of work was a steam-powered mobile generator that was used to drive saws and other equipment needed in the construction. (JF.)

Among the notable people that came to tour the construction of Camp Pike was Arkansas senator Joe T. Robinson, who is seen here posing by the car door in hat and tie. The Ford Model T being driven by a young soldier bore the label "U.S.A. Construction Q.M. [quartermaster] No. 1." (JF.)

At the height of construction, a million board feet of lumber arrived by train and wagons daily; it was taken to the work sites, where hundreds of workers assembled and raised the walls over floors already built. (JF.)

Among the workers building Camp Pike were 1,500 men from Puerto Rico, a US territory since the Spanish-American War less than 20 years earlier. Around 3,000 unskilled workers were also brought in from Texas and Oklahoma. (JF.)

In one of his reports to Washington, DC, Major Fordyce mentioned, "We did not have a single strike or serious disagreement during the entire project." He explained that he had made clear that the project was to be "an open shop," meaning union and nonunion labor had to work side by side. Fordyce went on to write, "This fact was made known to all workers, and any foreman found compelling a workman to join a union, or discharging him because he was not a member, was promptly placed in the guardhouse." (JF.)

Major Fordyce added on his enforcement of open shop laws in another report: "I at one time, I had the President of the Plumbers Union and at another, one of the heads of the Carpenters Union, in the guard house and only 'pardoned' them out upon their solemn promise to be loyal American citizens." (JF.)

Work on the many structures was sometimes measured by camera during the course of a day, as was the case of the barracks building here, photographed at early morning and again near day's end. On June 26, 1917, the word went out that the first building in Camp Pike was completed, with others to follow rapidly. (Both, JF.)

All the construction at Camp Pike did not rise above the ground; some, including water and sewer pipes, were buried beneath the earth. The photographer noted above that the men were placing wire-bound redwood pipe, a wood that would resist insects and decay. Below, hard manual labor went into the task of piecing the many miles of pipe together that crisscrossed Camp Pike. (Both, JF.)

"Kewanee Boiler Company 1917" was part of what was on the face of each coal-fired boiler being installed at Camp Pike; the boilers would help generate heat and some of the power needed by the sprawling camp. (JF.)

With millions of feet of lumber and much activity, the threat of fire was always a concern. The assigned fire brigade posed with their equipment during the construction in 1917. (JF.)

On September 5, 1917, Maj. John Fordyce telegraphed the US War Department: "Barracks available for 35,000 troops, lavatories for 20,000, quarters available for 800 officers. 10 quartermaster warehouses ready for use, 20,000 troops can be supported with 30 gallons of water per day." Two days later, the advance guard of a planned 40,000 men arrived at the camp. (JF.)

If counted as a city, the finished Camp Pike would have been among the largest in Arkansas when completed. It had 1,200 buildings and thousands of acres that had some 25 miles of road linking the facilities. The photograph above looked down one of the wide avenues between rows of barracks disappearing into horizon. The sign on the building to the right reads, "87th Division Exchange." (JF.)

Three

TRAINING TO GO "OVER THERE"

MEN AT DRILL, CAMP PIKE, LITTLE ROCK, ARK.

With Camp Pike finished, its mission to train doughboys swung into high gear, and draftees and volunteer enlistees poured in by the thousands. Marching was a required training exercise, a challenge for many of the new recruits.

Many of the new soldiers, both recruits and draftees, left their often small hometowns with great fanfare from the communities. The town of Paragould, in northeast Arkansas, turned out en masse to see off 120 local area boys leaving for Camp Pike to train for what was expected to be combat in France. (Courtesy Tom Mertens, Little Rock.)

OUR COUNTRY'S CALL

Are we ready to serve where'er it may be?
In our own beloved land, or over the sea?
To sacrifice all? Ah, the answer we know,
Is - Yes we are ready, ready to go,
With the highest of hopes and hearts beating true,
We are ready to die for the Red, White and Blue.

FRANK C. NELSON

GREETINGS

The patriotic fervor that gripped much of the country in the war with Germany was especially prominent in those enlisted, as reflected in a September 1917 postcard sent to Mary Measler of Marche, Arkansas. The sender wrote, "I stopped at church and services had started but I got there for the main part."

Posters like this were used to rally the nation as a whole but were especially directed at young men to entice them to join the Army and fight the Germans. The poster's theme played off the reported atrocities German troops committed on Belgium villages. Peaceful villages in the neutral country were razed, and many civilians were reportedly raped and executed.

The Selective Service Act, as the military draft was called, was enacted May 18, 1917. This authorized the federal government to, through conscription, raise an armed force for the war with Germany. Harry C. Lynn of Van Buren, Arkansas, got his draft board notice with orders to appear on February 6, 1918, for his physical exam.

NOTICE TO APPEAR FOR PHYSICAL EXAMINATION

Local Board for _____ Van Buren, Arkansas,

JAN 31 1918
(Date.)

You are hereby directed to appear before this Local Board for physical examination at 9 a.m. *on* FEB -6 1918
(Date)
Failure to do so is a misdemeanor, punishable by not to exceed one year's imprisonment, and may also result in your losing valuable rights and your immediate induction into military service.

FORM 1009—PMGO.
(See Sec. 122, S. S. R.)   c3—5138

Wallace Oliver
_____
Member of Local Board.

P. M. G. O. Form 65

Your Serial Number is __144__ *Order No.* __759__

Always refer to these numbers when writing.

BE ALERT Keep in touch with your Local Board
Notify Local Board immediately of change of address

3—5667

This will advise you that I got the
Board and have passed on your claim for deferment of call, and have excused you for a while
and you need not appear Friday.

Yours truly,

Claude Langley.

Lee Curtis Minor of Rabell, Arkansas, was perhaps relieved to get this draft board notice that indicated his request for a deferment from service had been passed on to review.

DRAFTED MEN ARRIVING AT CAMP PIKE, LITTLE ROCK, ARK.

Initially, the draft applied to men ages 21 to 30 but was amended in 1918 to include all men ages 18 to 45. Part of these draftees were among the men seen arriving at Camp Pike, still in civilian clothes and suitcases in hand, in this early 1918 image.

RECRUITS AT DRILL, CAMP PIKE, LITTLE ROCK, ARK.

The first wave of drafted men, around 10,000, arrived at Camp Pike in September 1917; another 17,000 were due three weeks later. Drill for the new men recently arrived at the camp began even before they were issued uniforms or weapons. The long line of soldiers was assembled in front of barracks under the eyes of their drill sergeants.

Days before arriving at Camp Pike, the drafted men had been farmers, shopkeepers, or laborers, but soon all would become soldiers in the United States Army. The men pictured, likely on the day of their arrival, had been issued rifles but were still clad in civilian attire, including a variety of hats. (Courtesy Ark Studies Institute.)

Local Board for Van Buren Co.,
Clinton, Arkansas.

This Certifies that _George D Morris_

Order No. _4_, Serial No. _904_, has been finally

classified and recorded in Class _1 a_

Hamp Bradley

FORM 1007.—PMGO
(See Sec. 110, S.S.R.)

Member of Local Board.
3—5121

George Morris, of Clinton, Arkansas, carried his draft card that showed his status as 1A. By the end of World War I, some two million men had volunteered while 2.8 million had been drafted.

Motherhood played a role in the recruiting of soldiers, as well, perhaps, as the draft. This sheet music cover shows an American mother offering up her son to the nation to fight the Germans.

After being outfitted in their uniforms, new soldiers often visited Ewing Photography in the Division Exchange opposite the train depot. The photographs of the new soldiers would be mailed home to family to be proudly passed around dining tables and front porches after the postman came.

Ewing Photography offered the American flag as a backdrop for a postcard to send home to the family. New soldiers were restricted to their barracks for 10 days to quarantine against infectious diseases. Only after this period were uniforms issued.

"Isn't he cute" was penned on the back of this postcard featuring a young soldier posing at Camp Pike, perhaps made to send home to a girl who promised to wait for him to return from wartime service.

A newly arrived soldier penned a note home on a postcard looking from the main camp entrance: "I got to camp all right and am feeling fine. It is 110 in the shade but the night am cool which makes it nice to sleep." These were the words of Adam Dangerfeld in August 1918.

CAMP PIKE LOOKING WEST FROM ENTRANCE, LITTLE ROCK, ARK.   222852

Penned on this postcard was "Harry & Army Chaplain, Camp Pike, Ark." Presumably, Harry is the young man on the left; both he and the chaplain were wearing their side arms outside a barracks building. According to one private's mail home, the new soldiers were issued two pairs of shoes, two woolen shirts, two pairs of pants, three pairs of socks, a belt, a hat, two woolen blankets, two towels, a toothbrush, soap, a pair of leggings, and a mess kit for dining.

An essential task in preparing to go to war was becoming proficient in the use of firearms. According to this postcard, the range, seen here hosting hundreds of soldiers, had the targets set 200 yards out.

#976—BARRACKS WHERE UNCLE SAM'S SOLDIERS LIVE.

The soldier who penned this postcard of a unit formed for drill in front of a barracks was apparently one trained on the machine guns. Writing to Pvt. Nels Olson at Camp Gordon, Georgia, he said, "Am in 4th A.N.G. [Arkansas National Guard] machine gun battalion."

MACHINE GUN RANGE, CAMP PIKE, ARK.

Machine guns were a new weapon of destruction that had been introduced by the Germans before the war, but new generations of more lethal guns came to the battlefields of Europe. Uncle Sam's soldiers were trained in the use of such weapons as preparation for the war against the Germans.

SQUAD DRILL, CAMP PIKE, LITTLE ROCK, ARK.   222769

Training with weapons was not all about the firing; it also included many drills to learn precision movements with fellow soldiers. A young solder, James Davenport, mailed this card in June 1918, writing, "I am not going to send my hat because it isn't any account. You can have my watch and carry it if you want. Got me a razor and outfit."

49

Long, hard hikes were a part of the training meant to toughen the young men after they arrived at Camp Pike, which made for quite a few sore feet. A young soldier, "Judd," wrote on this card to his aunt in New York: "Have been transferred to Camp Pike, here 2 weeks, climate is fine, well satisfied." The card was postmarked in November 1917; World War I would last another year.

At the end of a long hike, three soldiers were ready for a break at Water Station No. 2.

1987   Officer Giving the Boys the Guard Manual in Front of Barracks.

This image reads, "Officer giving the boys the Guard Manual in front of barracks," showcasing the officers' role in getting young men, who weeks earlier may have been store clerks or farmers, fit for Army service.

Part of the recruits' and draftees' training was to prepare for a new horror that had been introduced on the battlefields of Europe: chemical warfare, especially the use of chlorine and mustard gas. One of the soldiers at Camp Pike posed in a gas mask in front of a barracks in 1917.

A mass of seated troops was photographed while watching a training exercise in how to use smoke screens on the battlefield.

Digging fire trenches, communication trenches, and approach trenches

COPYRIGHT BY AMERICAN PRESS ASS'N

A noted part of the Camp Pike training for troops was the construction and preparation of trench warfare. Trenches were often dug in parallel lines—those in the front for facing the enemy, others farther back for supply purposes. The zigzag pattern seen in the trench to the left was made to limit damage in the case of artillery strikes.

On a cold day in the winter of 1917–1918, a group of visitors toured the practice trenches at Camp Pike. Three uniformed soldiers stand in the trench while talking with the well-dressed men in overcoats, at least one smoking a cigar.

A group of nurses from the Camp Pike base hospital posed in one of the training trenches. An estimated 200,000 soldiers from all sides died in the trenches of World War I, some from wounds, but others from disease brought on by the harsh conditions. The trenches were very unsanitary, often filled with rats; trench foot and dysentery were also common.

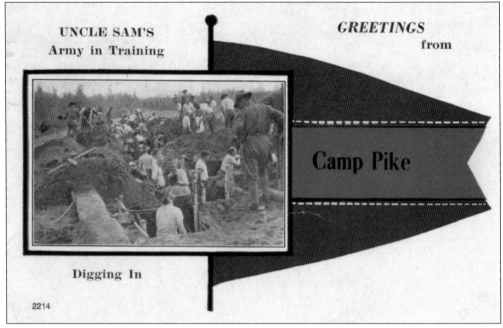

UNCLE SAM'S
Army in Training

GREETINGS
from

Camp Pike

Digging In

2214

"Uncle Sam's Army in training" and "Digging in" are printed on this postcard. A young Camp Pike soldier penciled on the back of the postcard, "The other side shows the way we dig up the earth, but have been playing ball today. Am on fire guard tonight."

School for Bakers and Cooks Camp Pike

The training at Camp Pike was not all in the art of war, but also about training men to meet the essential needs of the thousands of soldiers, including feeding them. The school for bakers was filled with young recruits learning the make the thousands of pounds of bread that would be consumed in the dining halls of Camp Pike. According to the post's YMCA, Camp Pike soldiers consumed 12 tons of bread a day.

Four

CAMP LIFE AND A
LITTLE R&R

Daily life at Camp Pike, aside from training, was frequently photographed and often shared on postcards. Views included a bound packet of postcards, upon which was pictured Maj. Gen. Samuel D. Sturgis, commander of the 87th Division of the Army, which had been activated at the camp in 1917. His father, also named Samuel, had been a Union general in the Civil War and a veteran of the Mexican and Indian wars. Commander Sturgis had a brother, Lt. James Sturgis, who died with General Custer's 7th Calvary Regiment at Little Big Horn in 1876. A young soldier at Camp Pike sent this postcard to Iowa in 1918, writing, "I am fine and dandy except pretty hot down in the rocks and sand."

Traffic entering or leaving Camp Pike had to pass through the entrance manned by twin stone guardhouses. On the day this photograph was made, traffic included a wagon bearing a load of hay. The stone guardhouses still stand today at the military-only entrance to Camp Robinson.

Remount Station, Camp Pike, Little Rock, Ark.

Hay was a necessary import into Camp Pike during World War I, as horses and mules played a role even in the now mechanized Army. Today, Remount Road is familiar to area residents near modern-day Camp Robinson, having been named for the area where the Army's horses were stabled.

A View of Camp Pike, Little Rock, Ark.

There were more horses than automobiles outside a Camp Pike barracks in this early-1918 photograph. Two horses were tethered to a tree, a mule was pulling a wagon past the lone auto, and another wagon was parked just beyond.

Penciled by a soldier named Albert to someone named Bessie, this card reads, "This shows our company tailor, we must keep our clothes all clean and mended. We have inspection every Saturday and if we aint up to date we get sentry duty or guard house."

CAMP PIKE
NEAR LITTLE ROCK, ARKANSAS

"Brother Al" mailed this four-frame folding postcard to his sister, writing, "Dear Sister, I tried to find my 'stable' as the boys call it but did not succeed. Anyhow they are all alike and this will show you what sort of houses we live in. If you see a number 617 on any building that is where I

The aerial view of a portion of the long wooden frame section of barracks was most likely taken from atop a water tower. Mailed by a soldier named Nick in October 1917, the message home to Louisiana read, "Sorry to hear Auntie was so sick, hope she will get better soon. I am well thank god. Getting fat up here. Heard some of our boys are in the trenches, hope we will be there soon so this war will end."

used to be then look criss-cross and this where I am now, I think 613. Each barracks is numbered in order 1-2-3-4 etc and is given a street number also (617)." The expanse of the card, looking top left to bottom right shows the enormity of Camp Pike, with a busy rail operation in the center.

A ground-level view of some of the barracks of Camp Pike could be seen from the main gate of the post; its twin stone guardhouses set along each side of the dirt street leading into the camp. To the right, beside the automobiles, was one of the buildings that housed businesses such as canteens and photographers that sprang up to serve thousands of soldiers going and coming from the camp.

The YMCA first demonstrated the nation's desire to see to the welfare of soldiers before the Civil War, and their work reached new levels during World War I. The YMCA employed a staff of 56 at Camp Pike, some in the buildings shown here. A solder wrote home, "Make sure all my clothes are taken care of because if ever get back I won't have much money to buy any because you don't make much here, but I got 40 bucks on me now."

INTERIOR Y. M. C. A., CAMP PIKE, LITTLE ROCK, ARK.

The YMCA facilities at Camp Pike offered the young soldiers a quiet retreat in which they could read or write letters home on stationery furnished by the facility staff. The YMCA reported that some nights it gave out as many as 20,000 pages of stationery. Each YMCA building had a post office. A brochure given to arriving soldiers said, "Here, around a blazing fire, the boys gather by the hundreds, day and night to swap years, read, write home or listen to phonograph."

The YMCA drew huge crowds one night for an outdoor showing of a silent Western movie. The organization gave arriving soldiers a brochure with a map showing eight locations at Camp Pike. The brochure said, "Testaments are distributed by the thousand, after quiet, earnest talks with the soldiers. Each building has a large wing with class rooms, library and reading room."

The American Library Association (ALA) was founded in Philadelphia in 1876 to promote the profession of librarian and to enhance learning for all. When the United States entered World War I in 1917, the association created a War Service Committee to distribute reading materials to soldiers. Working with the YMCA and the Red Cross, the ALA established 36 training camp libraries, including this one at Camp Pike.

WRITING HOME TO MOTHER AT K. OF C. BUILDING.

The Catholic men's organization known as the Knights of Columbus did its part for the troops training at Camp Pike. "Everyone welcome, Everything free" was the slogan for the Knights' clubhouses that were located on a number of World War I training bases; the organization gave out free stationery to be used for "writing home to mother."

Posters like this, showing a blessing being bestowed before going into battle, were likely on display in the Knights of Columbus buildings at Camp Pike. The camp locations afforded a chaplain that allowed Catholic soldiers to practice their faith. After the war, the Knights set up employment boards to assist returning soldiers.

INTERIOR OF BARRACKS. CAMP PIKE, LITTLE ROCK, ARK.

Sleeping accommodations within the many barracks buildings were spartan, with each soldier getting a cot and little space to store his gear. The frame buildings had no dry wall, carpet, or even paint. They were hot in the summer and could be cold in the winter.

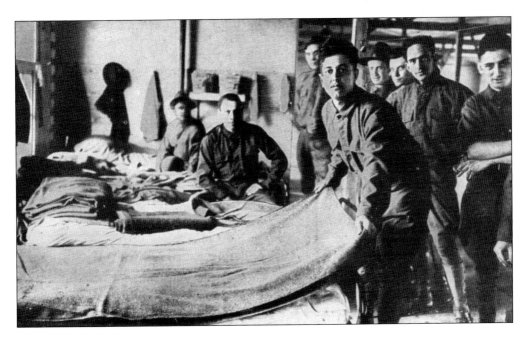

AIRING OUT, CAMP PIKE, ARK.

On occasion, the soldiers in training would be ordered to bring their beds and other belongings outside for an airing out. Each cot contained a single mattress filled with straw and covered with an olive green blanket.

HOTEL BELMONT, ADJOINING CAMP PIKE, LITTLE ROCK, ARK.

While living quarters for the enlisted soldiers were sparse, a number of officers, especially those with wives, lived in the Hotel Belmont. The Italian Renaissance–style building had opened adjacent to what would become Camp Pike in 1910. It was built by the Catholic Diocese to serve as St. Joseph's Orphanage and as recently as 1914 had been home to 300 children. The Army leased the building and 300 acres from the diocese for three years, converting the orphanage into lodging and naming it Hotel Belmont. The orphanage's chapel was, by some accounts, converted to a bar.

1978—MESS ROOM IN THE CANTONMENT BARRACKS.

Dining buildings at Camp Pike were busy as shifts of hungry young soldiers moved through after a hard day of training. Food was cooked en masse, usually consisting of a standard diet of low-grade beef, chicken, pork, beans, and potatoes.

A soldier named Magnus Nottwest mailed a comic postcard takeoff on the Army food to Minnesota in March 1918: "My Dear Miss Hodgson, A word to let you know I am still existing. Don't take this card too seriously, Its exaggerated in part at least. We are to be ready to leave in 90 days we are told. Write again."

The dinner fare for the officers of Headquarters Company of the 43rd Infantry likely was a bit above what the enlisted men found on their tables at Christmas dinner in 1917. The program booklet, bearing the flags of the United States, Britain, and France, contained the menu, which included oyster soup, roast turkey, chestnut dressing, five kinds of cake, coffee, cigars, cocoa, and cigarettes.

Dishwashing was usually done outside the barracks while standing on packed dirt between the buildings. The wooden, elevated walk to the left allowed access to the washing area, avoiding the sometimes muddy conditions.

Soldiers with a pass to leave the camp sometimes took one of the trains serving the training base. They most often went into Little Rock, but given enough leave, a number of the soldiers took the train to Hot Springs, Arkansas, some 50 miles to the southwest. The Missouri Pacific Railroad ticket shown was issued in March 1918.

These young soldiers rode the train into Little Rock and entertained three well-dressed young women on the lawn of City Park. In the photograph below, one soldier seems to be giving his lady companion a ride on one of the park's mowing machines.

Troops with a day or two of leave often took the train to Hot Springs, a Victorian-era spa given federal protection because of its thermal mineral springs, which was only a short ride of less than two hours away. These soldiers posed at the Happy Hollow Photography Studio, located at the foot of Hot Springs Mountain behind the Arlington Hotel.

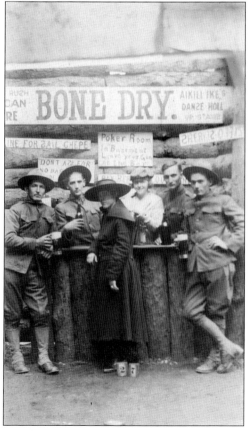

Four young soldiers on leave posed at the "bone dry" display at the Happy Hollow studio, pretending to drink beer. As this was during the Prohibition era, the drinking, or even possession, of alcohol would have been illegal. However, few vices were off limits in the spa city, including gambling and prostitution, where brothels operated openly. The Camp Pike commander told the Hot Springs mayor to shutdown the brothels or he would ban soldiers from taking leave in the city. The mayor merely ordered the brothels to keep a lower profile.

While on leave to Hot Springs, one soldier visited the ostrich farm, a popular attraction in the resort city. Visitors were allowed to pose atop the huge birds, in this case with a bag over the ostrich's head so as not to frighten the creature.

Back at Camp Pike, soldiers found chances closer to their barracks for photo postcards, including this one in which the uniformed man is posed "flying" over the camp.

A soldier named Arthur wrote the following on February 21, 1918, "This is the picture of two Mich. Boys and the one I suppose you know." The men from Michigan and Arthur are posed atop an iconic Arkansas symbol, "On the HOG in Arkansas"

The horses and mules that had been important in the building and early operations of Camp Pike had been largely replaced by fleets of trucks, some of which are shown here. Mechanically skilled men were essential to keeping the vehicles running in training, just as they would be on the supply lines behind the battlefields.

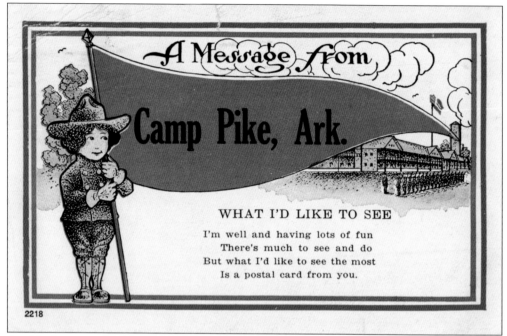

A soldier's message to Emilie Jabel of Montello, Wisconsin, written 12 days before Christmas 1917, spoke of a lonely man, likely writing while sitting on a cot in a cold, drafty barracks. "I still think and wish I was with you for Christmas but they want leave. I had a letter from Perry asking me what I wanted for Christmas and all that I want is my freedom, that is all I ask Dear. Believe me Dear I miss my good times, will close for this sermon."

During the long winter of 1917–1918, one popular postcard in the Camp Pike Post Exchange (PX) was this one, portraying a soldier reflecting on the timeless Christmas image of the three wise men following the star to Bethlehem.

Five

HEALTH CARE AND SHIPPING OUT

BASE HOSPITAL, CAMP PIKE, LITTLE ROCK, ARK.

Thousands of soldiers in rigorous training for all manner of weapons crowding together in drafty barracks in an era before of antibiotics was a challenge for training bases like Camp Pike. A base hospital with trained personnel was a vital part of Camp Pike and was well documented in photographs. The postcard above shows the hospital complex on the left in a series of long wooden buildings.

Army nurses were vital to caring for injured and ill soldiers, both at Camp Pike and in field hospitals in France. When the United States entered World War I, the Army had around 4,000 active duty nurses, all women, as it was then considered an exclusively female profession. By the end of the war, the number had surpassed 20,000. The nurses serving at Camp Pike lived in cottages that lined one of the dirt roads on the post.

Nurses Quarters with Club House for Nurses #1
Base Hospital - Camp Pike, Ark.

When off duty, some of the nurses enjoyed horseback riding on the grounds of the sprawling Camp Pike, no doubt drawing a lot of interest from the thousands of young soldiers as they passed on horseback. No Army nurses were killed in combat during World War I, though 3 were wounded by shellfire and 272 died of disease, primarily pneumonia, tuberculosis, and influenza.

Nurses' recreational facilities were well appointed, allowing them to enjoy a break with coffee or tea. The quarters would have been decidedly off limits to the thousands of young soldiers training elsewhere on the sprawling base.

During World War I, an estimated 30 percent of the nation's doctors were in military service. Dr. Ida Josephine Brooks overcame the obstacles of gender by getting into medical school in Boston after being refused admission in Little Rock, forging a trail for other women. Dr. Brooks was denied enlisting in the military at the start of the war but was able to obtain a commission with the US Public Health Service, which stationed her at Camp Pike.

Dr. Brooks, pictured here later in life, served at the camp as a consultant in psychiatry with the rank of assistant surgeon. After the war, Dr. Brooks served as a psychiatrist of Little Rock City Schools and was instrumental in establishing a school for "mentally deficient" students. She died in Little Rock in 1939.

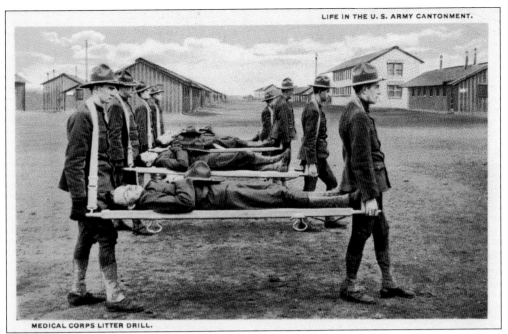

MEDICAL CORPS LITTER DRILL.

Training for enlisted men serving in the Army medical teams included the medical corps litter drill, an exercise that would be used all too often on overseas battlefields.

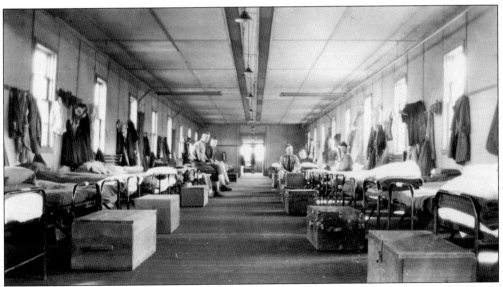

"Medical Dept Barracks" was penciled on this 1918 Camp Pike photograph. By the end of World War I, the US Army had more than 30,000 medical officers, including 350 African American doctors, and 250,000 enlisted men working in the training camp hospitals and in combat units on the war fronts.

This image is labeled "Bright and attractive medical ward;" it shows a ward that included a record player, seen on the right. By the end of the war, the Army's medical department had increased its total hospital bed capacity in the United States from 9,500 to 120,000.

This "splendidly equipped orthopedic dept" was a proud feature of the Camp Pike hospital. Orthopedics would see significant advancements in the coming years due to necessity, as terrible wounds from machine guns and shell fragments were inflicted upon soldiers on the battlefields of France.

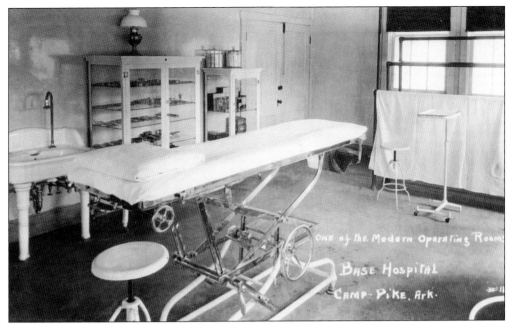

Soldiers in need of surgery benefited from modern, well-equipped operating rooms in Camp Pike's hospital buildings.

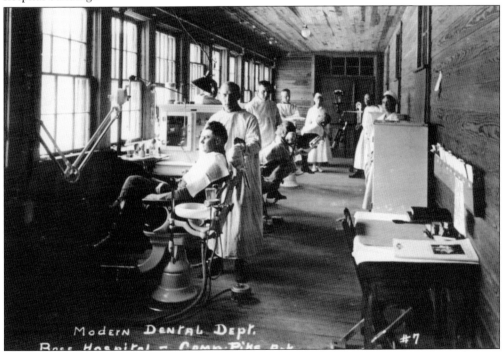

Thousands of soldiers equaled many thousands of teeth in an age before fluoride or orthodontics, which kept the dental clinic at Camp Pike busy. Congress passed a bill in 1916 to organize the Army Dental Corps. By November 1918, a total of 4,620 dentists were at work in the Army, Army Reserve, and National Guard. During the war, Army dentists performed some two million procedures; eight dental officers died in combat. (NARA.)

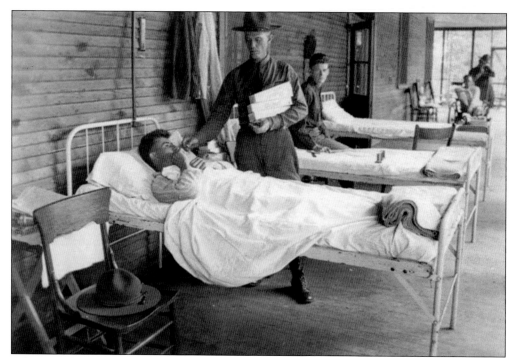

Fifty years before the US Surgeon General confirmed cigarettes were deadly, the US Army distributed tobacco products as readily as it did food and medicine. A medical personnel soldier was photographed helping an injured, bedfast soldier smoke while holding three cartons of cigarettes under his arm. The beds for the smoking soldiers had apparently been moved onto the screened porches of the Camp Pike hospital.

The screened porches of the Camp Pike's hospital buildings were often used by convalescent soldiers. One in the background is confined to his bed, another his wheelchair.

Food production for the sometimes hundreds of soldiers hospitalized at Camp Pike took planning. The hospital kept its own herd of dairy cattle to meet the nutritional needs of its patients.

Hospitalized soldiers consumed a significant amount of bread, which was baked on-site at the hospital's facilities.

Black Americans played a role in the training at Camp Pike for World War I, but for the most part, these men were relegated to kitchen duty and other manual labor instead of being trained for combat. The hardworking men shown here were assigned to the Camp Pike officers' dining halls where they cooked and served the officers who would have all been white.

The medical profession of occupational therapy (OT) grew significantly due to the needs of injured and wounded soldiers in World War I. The National Society for OT, formed in 1917, persuaded the US Army to hire 5,000 reconstruction aides to provide OT to wounded soldiers. One of Camp Pike's occupational therapists had her patients outside while learning to embroider as a way to regain the use of their hands.

Occupational Therapists are shown teaching patients how to weave baskets and build toys. Before the war, the general philosophy had been to only bestow charity upon the crippled. Using OT, that philosophy shifted to a belief that it was wiser to equip the patients with skills that would enable them to function socially and hopefully become employable.

By May 1918, the Army used occupational therapists to teach crafts on the wards to patients who had impaired motor function or who were neurotic or mentally disoriented. Gradually, the occupational therapists assumed more responsibility for curative activities. The therapist shown on this postcard is giving instructions in weaving.

Physical and mental health conditions sometimes led to prolonged stays at Camp Pike's hospital facilities. To keep the men busy and to help them gain skills that might later prove useful, there were are variety of vocational training programs offered to the soldiers. Motor mechanics is the subject seen here. In the center of the photograph are two African American soldiers at work; the hospital classes brought black and white soldiers together long before an integrated military.

The convalescent soldiers here are learning type setting, a skilled trade in the decades before computerized word processors.

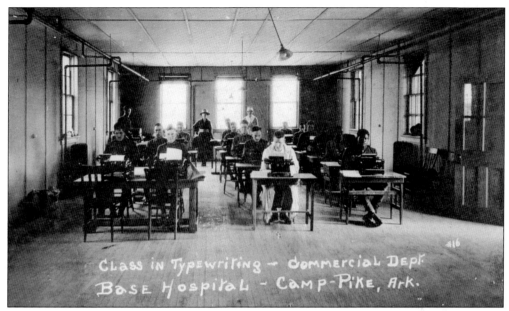

The women in the rear of the room are teaching soldiers, including the one in the center wearing a robe, to type. Notable is the presence of a black soldier to the right, some 30 years before the Army was integrated.

The greatest health challenge within the crowded barracks of Camp Pike, where many thousands of men could be stationed at a time, was the arrival of the Spanish influenza virus in the fall of 1918. The flu strain that would kill 22 million worldwide slammed the Army post hard. The soldiers in training feel ill at a rate of a 1,000 a day; so many died that Camp Pike's commanders stopped publishing obituary notices. The camp was quarantined for a time. (ANGM.)

SOLDIERS READY TO LEAVE CAMP PIKE, LITTLE ROCK, ARK.   222846

The soldiers' training eventually ended, and many prepared to ship out. In all, 72,000 Arkansans served in World War I, including 1,400 women and 18,000 African Americans. According to the *Encyclopedia of Arkansas*, 2,183 of those from the state that served died, half from illness, while 1,751 were injured. These postcards show the trained soldiers lined up and seated by the tracks waiting on the train to take them to ship out for what could be the battlefields of France.

SOLDIERS WAITING FOR TRAIN TO LEAVE, CAMP PIKE, LITTLE ROCK, ARK.   222844

At least one soldier from Paragould, Arkansas, would not make it safely back home. Pvt. Ranzie Adams, who was 23 years old at the time, trained at Camp Pike and shipped out to France in April 1918, vowing to his mother, "I will give the last drop of my blood for my country, gladly, before I would see those Huns overrun our land and deal with you and sister as they have with women in Belgium and France."

Private Adams was killed on the western front of France on May 28, 1918, little more than a month after arriving in France. The headlines of the Paragould paper read, "Spirit of Ranzie Adams Wafted into Eternity Through the Sacred Folds of Old Glory." His mother said, "It nearly breaks my heart to lose my boy. To have died so far from us and his home, but I am glad to given him for his country. Glad that he had the strong heart, courage and honor to volunteer." Private Adams's remains lie in the Browns Chapel Cemetery, outside Paragould, Arkansas.

The fate of Camp Pike was up in the air after the war ended in November 1918. It was used first as a center to process demobilized troops and even as Camp Pike College, using the support of the Knights of Columbus to train men for civilian careers. The camp also served as a center to rehabilitate wounded soldiers, especially those who had lost limbs in combat. By 1921, however, the US Army was done with the base, passing it into the hands of the state to train the Arkansas National Guard. In the 1930s, it would become a branch of the Civilian Conservation Corps, serving men such as the three young members pictured here, all from Ohio.

By the 1930s, the unoccupied barracks built in such haste in 1917 were rapidly deteriorating, beginning to fall victim to the elements and a peacetime America in which the citizens hoped there would never again be a need for such a massive military training camp. This would, sadly, be a false hope, as an even greater world war was looming on the horizon.

Six

CAMP ROBINSON IN SERVICE TO THE NATION

When the US Army shuttered Camp Pike and its training mission in 1922, it deeded 6,480 acres to the State of Arkansas with the provision it be used primarily for military purposes and, if ever needed, the federal government could reclaim the land. Some facilities that had served for World War I became a training base for the Arkansas National Guard, but the coming of a second world war would invoke the clause that let the federal government reclaim the base. Greatly expanded, it became Camp McRae then Camp Robinson and trained many thousands of soldiers for the worldwide conflict. The Camp Robinson soldier pictured above around 1941 epitomized the nation's intent to preserve liberty.

The former Camp Pike, designated to serve the Arkansas National Guard, was renamed Camp McRae in the 1920s (before becoming Camp Robinson). The assets were sold off with the proceeds used to build a home for the Arkansas National Guard. The renaming was to honor Thomas McRae, who served as Arkansas's governor from 1921 to 1925. Among McRae's other accomplishments was creating a tuberculosis sanitarium for African Americans and making women eligible for civil service appointments.

By the 1930s, many of the World War I–era barracks of the former Camp Pike had deteriorated beyond repair. Almost all were torn down for salvage, with the proceeds going to support the new guard facilities. The Arkansas National Guardsmen training at Camp McRae were, in many cases, housed in tents.

In August 1937, Camp McRae became Camp Joseph T. Robinson to honor the former congressman, governor, senator, and 1928 vice presidential nominee. Robinson had died the previous month of a heart attack. This postcard was mailed to Missouri in 1942 by Pvt. Melvin Mitchell with the message, "I don't think the army is going to be so bad after all."

In contrast to the tents seen in the photograph on the opposite page, the Camp Robinson Administration Building was a solid structure. The message on this 1938 postcard reads, "Here's where the payoff happens and the scandal sheets on all the officers are maintained." Barney, the man who wrote this, was apparently an enlisted man housed in one of the tents.

Soldiers training at Camp Robinson in the late 1930s wore uniforms and used weapons left over from the World War I era. The field gun in action here was mounted on wooden spoke wheels in a carriage that was likely built to be drawn by horses but later adapted to be pulled by a truck.

The US Army, with World War II already under way in Europe and Asia, reclaimed Camp Robinson in 1940, invoking the clause that had occurred when Camp Pike was given over to the state in 1922. The camp was first envisioned as a tent-barracks containment for 25,000 soldiers. All troops, except general officers, were housed in the tent structures.

In preparation for a likely war, Camp Robinson was expanded to 44,000 acres in late 1940. The camp was largely composed of tents until after Pearl Harbor's attack in December 1941. By the middle of 1942, the camp was made up of 6,763 buildings, more than 5,000 of these "hutments," which replaced the tents. The enlisted men's shelters, some seen being assembled, were placed on a 16-by-16-foot wooden floor; the bottom half of the hutments had wooden siding while the top half was screened and had canvas flaps. They had but a single electric outlet and were heated by a gas stove. The hutments were perched upon concrete cinder blocks and served their purpose, but after the war, they were removed when the camp scaled down in peacetime. (NARA.)

The 35th Division of the US Army began arriving at Camp Robinson in January 1941. Made up of National Guard units from Kansas, Missouri, and Nebraska, the 35th Division would spend most of the year at Camp Robinson. When Pearl Harbor was attacked in December, the division was rushed to California to provide coastal defense. "Sure enjoy this even if it is almost 24 hour a day job," wrote a soldier in an August 1941 note to California.

35th. DIV. MASSED COLORS
CAMP ROBINSON, ARK. #13

The aerial view of the 35th Division's facilities, among other portions of Camp Robinson, showed what a sprawling presence the military post was taking on in advance of the United States' entry into World War II.

Aerial View 35th Division - Camp Robinson, Ark.

35th Division Rifle Range - Camp Robinson, Ark.

Despite the fact that the United States would not formally enter World War II until December 1941, training for thousands of solider was well under way by the time of this May 1941 postcard featuring the 35th Division rifle range. In a message home to St. Louis, one soldier wrote, "Here's a card of our rifle range, I am feeling fine."

35th Division Rifle Range - Camp Robinson, Ark.

The soldiers of the 35th Division practice their marksmanship in the prone position using rifles.

35th Division Pistol Range - Camp Robinson, Ark.

The 35th Division sought proficiency on the pistol range as well as the rifle range. The drawn arrow was pointed at William R. Bryant of the 140th Infantry of the 35th Division, who penned in March 1941, "Freda, this picture was taken of us using the .45 caliber pistol."

10th Engineers - 35th Division - Camp Robinson, Ark.

The 10th Engineers of the 35th Division honed the skill of building pontoon bridges that would get men and equipment over a stream or lake. It would be a skill in high demand in Europe, where many bridges were knocked out by artillery and bombers.

The men of the 35th Division at Camp Robinson were trained to be able to rapidly scale telephone poles.

"This is a smoke screen, I am on my knees by the gun," reads a March 27, 1941, note from a soldier training with the 35th Division; the division wore World War I–era helmets and used small, wooden carriage artillery, likely a antitank gun, that was already very obsolete.

95th Div. Telephone Pole Climbing Inst., Camp Robinson, Arkansas.

35th Division Anti Tank Gun Crew & Infantrymen. Camp Robinson, Ark.

In December 1941, with the shock of the attack on Pearl Harbor still in the headlines, the 35th Division shipped out of Camp Robinson, bound for San Luis Obispo, California, to provide coastal defense. The well-trained men of the 35th would not stay stateside forever, sailing to England in May 1944. The division landed on Omaha Beach in July 1944 and saw heavy combat while fighting off German counterattacks. The division would later spearhead attacks into the German heartland. (ANGM.)

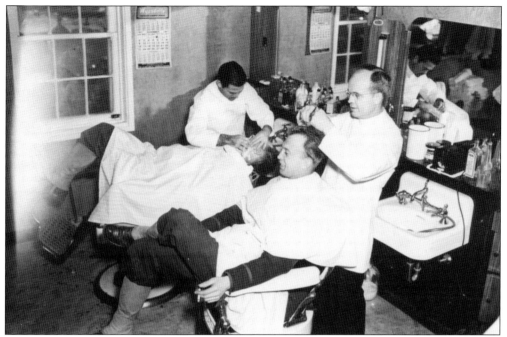

Ten days after the attack on Pearl Harbor, the chairs of Camp Robinson's barbershops were full and the talk was of the nation's entry into World War II but a few days earlier. The barbers are, from left to right, Charles Endicott from Kansas, shaving Pvt. A.M. Shoadon from Minnesota, and Gilbert Woddridge of Kansas, cutting the hair of Lt. Eugene Luche from North Dakota. (NARA.)

Other units quickly filled the training facilities in the wake of the 35th Division's shift to the West Coast. Cpl. Al Baisie, who before the war had played for the Chicago Bears, was a member of the 101st Training Battalion. Instead of a defensive line, the corporal was hitting a bayonet dummy in practice for a Independence Day demonstration. (NARA.)

In March 1942, Capt. John Andie administered the oath of allegiance to a group of newly inducted men who had passed their Army physical. They would next be given serial numbers and service records. The photographer captured the name of one inductee—Elijah Kinkle of Square Meadows, Arkansas—but failed to indicate where he was in the image.

In January 1942, the Signal Photographic Company at Camp Robinson was in a trench, watching antitank batteries blast away at tank replicas. (ANGM.)

These recruits had only been in the Army for three weeks, but they were already working on their marksmanship on this cold February day in 1942, less than three months after the United States entered World War II. (NARA.)

Private Porter of Mound City, Missouri, was photographed honing his marksmanship skills. The private, of the 63rd Battalion, 13th Regiment, was demonstrating the kneeling position, one of four basic stances drilled into the riflemen. (ANGM.)

Pvt. Hiroshi Tanoate from Ault, Colorado, served with Company A, 63rd Battalion, 13th Regiment; he is seen here loading rifle ammunition into clips for disposition to men training on the firing lines. The private, of Japanese descent, was 22 years old and was inducted at Camp Roberts, California, in March 1942.

Private Holt came from Washington, DC, to train at Camp Robinson. In June 1942, he was photographed loading machine gun drums by candlelight in a dugout. (NARA.)

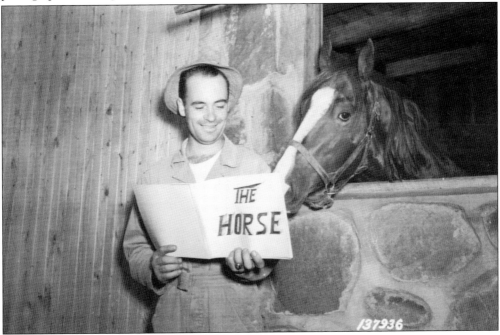

Life at Camp Robinson during World War II was not solely hard work; it included moments of levity. Pvt. Louie Morris of the Quartermasters' detachment station posed with a steed, reading a book entitled *The Horse*. The Quartermasters had previously handled only mechanized equipment but received a group of horses for the post in June 1942. (NARA.)

The Army really did move on its stomach, and Camp Robinson was no exception. The bakery turned out thousands of loaves of bread daily to feed as many as 50,000 hungry soldiers. The two men standing and inspecting the loaves in the image are identified as Sgt. Dewitt Hungerford of Canton, Kansas, left, and S.Sgt. Roy Schnarr of Duluth, Minnesota. The 9,000-square-foot bakery provided bread for the 149 mess halls on the base. (NARA.)

One of the 149 Camp Robinson mess halls was busy in the spring of 1942, with mashed potatoes and fried chicken on the menu, along with an ample supply of rolls from the camp's bakery. (NARA.)

Pres. Franklin Roosevelt proclaimed April 6, 1942, as Army Day, saying, "Our Army is a mighty arm of the tree of liberty. It is a living part of the American tradition, a tradition that goes back to Israel Putnam, who left his plow in a New England furrow to take up a gun and fight at Bunker Hill." Four Camp Robinson soldiers of Japanese descent are seen producing posters to advertise Army Day and welcome the local public to visit the post; a hundred of the posters were distributed in Little Rock. (NARA.)

Before enlisting, George Shayler worked for Kodak in Rochester, New York. Wartime found him operating a Mitchell camera in the field at Camp Robinson, part of the training given an Army motion picture cameraman. (NARA.)

A year after proclaiming Army Day, President Roosevelt, as a part of a war plant tour, came to visit Camp Robinson on Palm Sunday, April 18, 1943. Despite a cold, drizzling rain, FDR rode through the camp with the top down on his Packard, which traveled by train wherever the president went. Below, Arkansas governor Ben Laney is at the camp to greet the president. (NARA.)

On a hot June day in 1942, 1st Sgt. M.J. Stock, to the left of the tent, and Sgt C.L. Hamm of the 808th Tank Destroyer Battalion, to the right, were standing at attention while the field equipment for enlisted personnel was inspected by Capt A.S. Kilborn, far left, and Lt. E.N. Palmer. (NARA.)

The business of training for war never abated in 1942 at Camp Robinson, as seen in this March 9, 1942, image. Sgt. Newton Butler of Hope, Arkansas, has just parried the bayonet thrust of Pvt. Joseph Lackovitch of Ironwood, Michigan, and is gripping the rifle in preparation for disarming his opponent, a skill that could save his life on the battlefield. These soldiers were part of Company A, 63rd Battalion, 13th Regiment. (NARA.)

A refuge from the firing ranges and drill sergeants could be found at the new chapel, which was dedicated in November 1941. The soldiers pictured here are leaving dedication services at the new house of worship. During World War II, there were a total of 10 chapels spread over Camp Robinson. (NARA.)

The post's chapel was the site of the nuptials of Lt. Richard Melcher and his new wife, Carolyn Cavender, in late 1941. (NARA.)

Black soldiers, some from Northern states, were sent to Camp Robinson in what was still a very segregated US military; it would not be integrated until 1948. Most of the black soldiers were relegated to jobs such as driving trucks and other manual labor. The two soldiers here are at work in the machine shop of the camp's truck facility. Only late in the war would African American soldiers be sent into combat, where some 700 died. (NARA.)

This map of Greater Little Rock was printed in the 1943 *Handbook of Information* for the replacement training centers at Camp Robinson. It attempted to show what areas of Little Rock and North Little Rock were open to white soldiers and which were restricted to only black soldiers.

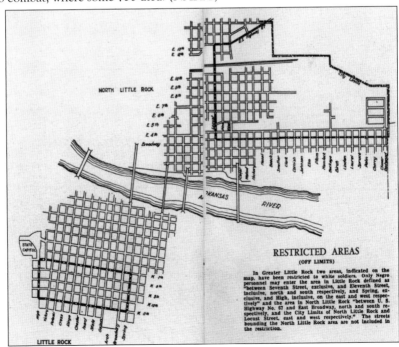

RESTRICTED AREAS
(OFF LIMITS)

In Greater Little Rock two areas, indicated on the map, have been restricted to white soldiers. Only Negro personnel may enter the area in Little Rock defined as "between Seventh Street, exclusive, and Eleventh Street, inclusive, north and south respectively, and Spring, inclusive, and High, inclusive, on the east and west respectively" and the area in North Little Rock "between U. S. Highway No. 67 and East Broadway, north and south respectively, and the City Limits of North Little Rock and Locust Street, east and west respectively." The streets bounding the North Little Rock area are not included in the restriction.

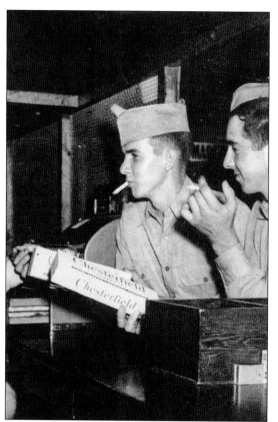

In 1943, American cigarette makers rolled out 290 billion cigarettes, with many being consumed by soldiers like these at the Camp Robinson Post Exchange (PX), where an entire carton cost as little as a dollar. Cigarettes were even a part of the GI's rations and were distributed freely by the Red Cross.

The advertisement for Camels ran in the weekly *Camp Robinson News*, promoting how a Camel pleased the "T-zone," the taste and throat, of the soldier. Cigarette consumption in the United States jumped a reported 75 percent between 1940 and 1945. The nation would pay a terrible toll in health care cost and premature deaths in the decades to come. (ANGM.)

Seven

FAMOUS VISITORS, WOMEN IN SERVICE, POWS, AND HONORING SACRIFICE

Gen. "Vinegar Joe" Stilwell paid a visit to the troops training at Camp Robinson in March 1945. The decorated general acquired his nickname for his caustic wit and salty language. Late in World War II, Stilwell commanded the forces in China and India, attempting to keep the Chinese in the war against the Japanese. He was recalled from China by President Roosevelt in October 1944. (NARA.)

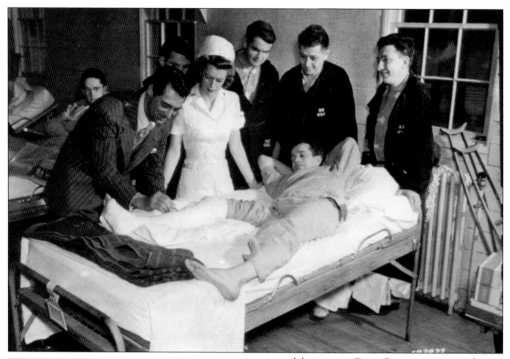

Movie star Cary Grant, a native of Great Britain who had been born Archibald Alexander Leach, visited Camp Robinson's hospital on March 20, 1943, signing a patient's cast under the watchful eye of a nurse and other patients. Grant tried to enlist in the British navy at the start of the war but was told he was too old. He donated some of his World War II movie salaries to American and British war efforts. (NARA.)

Jackie Cooper, an actor who won an Oscar at the age of nine, came to visit the troops at Camp Robinson early in the war, taking a turn at "KP." Cooper served in the Navy in the South Pacific toward the end of the war and spent many years afterwards in the naval reserves. When he died in 2011, he was buried at Arlington National Cemetery in honor of his military service. (NARA.)

The Women's Auxiliary Army Corps (WAAC) was formed in 1942, in part to do the work of men in the Army, who could then be freed up for combat. A WAAC recruiting center opened in Little Rock, and women who enlisted proved they were up to the jobs assigned, including overseas duty. Lt. Martha Rector, left, and Lt. Manice Hill, right, both from the Little Rock recruiting center, came to Camp Robinson to congratulate the new camp commander, Col. Grover Graham. The "auxiliary" term was dropped in 1943, leading the abbreviation to become WAC. (NARA.)

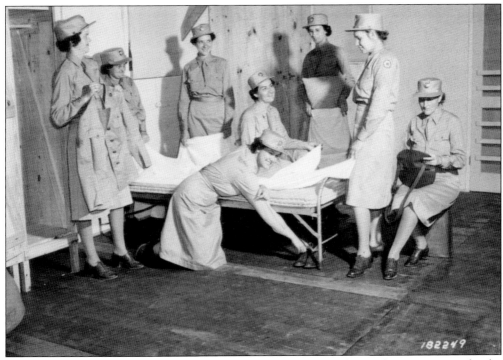

The members of the first WAC to recruit at Camp Robinson had some levity in posing for the camera while purporting to have a tidy bunk in June 1943. Basic training for the WACs was eight weeks, closely following that of men, with a lot of exercise, close order drill, and a 5.5-day workweek. By the end of the war, women had proven themselves proficient in 239 different Army jobs. The WACs were discontinued in 1978, when men and women began to serve together. (NARA.)

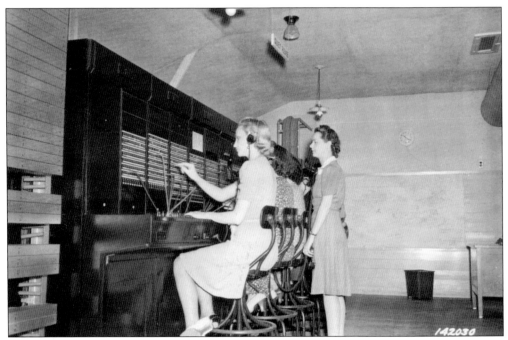

Civilian women also served at Camp Robinson, filling roles that freed enlisted men and women to do other important work. Irma Harris of Little Rock, standing, supervises civil service employees operating the main switchboard at the Signal Office of the 19th Signal Service Company in April 1942. (NARA.)

Some of the most welcome visitors at Camp Robinson were Ada Leonard and the All-American Girl Revue, who came in February 1942 to serve dinner to the men of the 162nd Signal Photographic Company. The "waitresses" were identified as, from left to right, Miss Sawyer, Miss Slade, Miss Swan, and Miss Leonard. (NARA.)

MOTHER

M is for the million things she gave me
O means only that she's growing old
T is for the tears she shed to save me
H is for her heart of purest gold
E is for her eyes with lovelight shining
R means right and right she'll always be

Put them all together, they spell

MOTHER

A word that means the world to me.

CAMP
JOS. T. ROBINSON
ARK.

Aside from pretty women who came to entertain the troops, a woman that was never far from the hearts and minds of many soldiers was their mother. A popular item at the local PX was a souvenir pillow bearing a poem ending with "Mother, A word that means the world to me."

A mother, or perhaps a girlfriend back home, was the recipient of this framed photograph of a young soldier in his dress uniform. Note the stars and stripes on either side of the frame.

GOD BLESS AMERICA

.CAMP ROBINSON

Pvt. Christian Zeissler, at right, had worries other than the women in his life. He was a newly drafted soldier in December 1941 who was discussing with regimental personnel officer Lt. Richard Hale a perplexing issue. The lieutenant was advising Private Zeissler that technically he was an alien and not entitled to Army pay, rations, or uniforms. The Russian native had been brought to the United States at the age of eight months but had never obtained citizenship papers. There is no record of how the problem was resolved. (ANGM.)

In February 1942, the citizens of the small town of Heber Springs, Arkansas, about 60 miles north of Camp Robinson, opened their homes for a weekend to the soldiers who rode the bus into the small mountain town. The weekend of soft beds, home cooked meals, parties, and the attention of pretty local girls was said to have been a most pleasant break for the soldiers in training. (ANGM.)

Camp Robinson's soldiers were out in force for a Memorial Day parade on May 30, 1942. This formation of troops was photographed by someone atop city hall as they marched across the Broadway Bridge, high over the Arkansas River. (NARA.)

In 1943, Armistice Day, today called Veterans Day, saw another parade turning off Main Street onto Capitol Avenue. The photograph, taken by the Signal Corps at Camp Robinson, carried commentary: "Their helmets symbolic of the might of America's fighting men, the 757th Railway Shop Battalion . . . show their smart lines of march to the thousands who thronged the streets of downtown Little Rock." (NARA.)

Health care was a major operation at Camp Robinson during World War II, with as many as 50,000 soldiers on the base on any given day. The camp had a 1,000-bed hospital, the largest in the state, with 36 wards connected by over 1.5 miles of covered walkways. (NARA.)

Many steps on the 1.5 miles of walkways between the 36 wards of the Camp Robinson hospital were covered by the officers of the Army Nurses Corps Social Club, which was formed by the women serving on the base. The club was a social group that organized bingo parties, dances, and other entertainment. Shown here from left to right are Pres. Celeste LeBlond of Sioux City, Iowa; Vice Pres. Mary Smiles of Waterloo, Iowa; Dorothy Cox of Doniphan, Iowa; and O.A. McCoy of Lincoln, Nebraska. (NARA.)

Christmas 1941 found the patients at the Camp Robinson base hospital entertained at the Red Cross Christmas party. The men are fixated on the face and voice of Joyce Wilson, who is playing the accordion and singing. (NARA.)

A medical replacement training center operated at Camp Robinson from 1942 to 1944, its purpose to train soldiers as medical personnel. Above, medical trainees are practicing removing a wounded soldier from a replica of a damaged tank. (NARA.)

For the first time since the Civil War, the United States established more than 500 prisoner of war camps on its soil. Camp Robinson became home to about 4,000 German POWs beginning in 1943, most from Erwin Rommel's North Afrika Korps, where they were captured. There was no longer room for them in England, and the continent was still controlled by the Nazis. The POWs above spent many hours building a model of a castle familiar to them from their homeland; it was made of rocks and gravel picked up in the camp. (NARA.)

It did not go unnoticed by the German POWs that the food found on their prison tables was better than they recalled having while fighting in Europe and North Africa. POWs were required to work around the camp and were even loaned out for civilian labor outside the camp. The prisoners were paid on average 80¢ a day for their labor, which allowed them to buy toiletries, candy, cigarettes, and even beer on the base. (NARA.)

At least four German prisoners died during their time at Camp Robinson, all from natural causes. Pictured is the funeral of Richard Jasker in a small plot set aside on the base for a POW cemetery. After the war, the remains of the prisoners were removed to the Fort Sam Houston's US military cemetery in Texas. (NARA.)

The German POWs were able to obtain their own Camp Robinson matches, labeled "Prisoner of War." One side of the matchbook cover bore a wishful image of a POW sailing away from the United States toward Hamburg, Germany.

EXTRA

The
Camp Robinson News

EXTRA

Volume 5

CAMP ROBINSON, ARKANSAS, AUGUST 14, 1945

Number 15

WAR ENDS

★ ★ ★ ★ ★ ★ ★ ★ ★ ★ ★ ★ ★ ★

LITTLE SONS OF HEAVEN
AGREE TO ALLIED TERMS

The long-awaited headline ran in the *Camp Robinson News* on August 14, 1945: the war was over with the surrender of Japan. During the preceding five years, some 750,000 men and women had trained at Camp Robinson to help win the largest conflict in history. Approximately 195,000 Arkansans served in the military during World War II, about 10 percent of the state's population. Approximately 3,500 died in the conflict. The casualty number among those who trained at Camp Robinson is unknown. (NARA.)

Just as thousands entered service at Camp Robinson, many would receive their discharge papers there after the war's end. The return to civilian life was captured in a photograph upon the discharge of Sgt. Harry S. Truman, a nephew of the president of the United States. Sergeant Truman, a veteran of the 44th Division Field Artillery, served 33 months, including overseas duty. His bag packed, he was heading home to his farm near Grandview, Missouri. (NARA.)

The war claimed brave men and women who died for their country, leaving loved ones to mourn but also cherish their memory. Col. Grover Graham, a Camp Robinson commander, posthumously awarded the Silver Star to Mary Schuller of 1710 Maryland Avenue in Little Rock for the heroism of her husband, Cpl. Paul Schuller, who served more than four years in the Army before dying in the Battle of Luzon in the Philippines on June 20, 1945. (NARA.)

In December 1945, Col. Grover Graham, Camp Robinson commander, was privileged to present Sgt. Albert Greer Jr. the Bronze Star for meritorious action against the enemy at Luzon in 1945. Though classified as a chief clerk not normally working near the front, Sergeant Greer had assumed responsibilities of receiving and preparing seriously wounded casualties for surgery in close proximity to the enemy. (NARA.)

In 1946, Gen. R.F. Reinhardt presented the Congressional Medal of Honor at the Arkansas's state capitol to a Mrs. Will Terry for her son Lt. Seymour Terry, who died in combat in Okinawa in 1945. Lieutenant Terry braved hails of bullets while running directly into enemy fire to secure satchel charges that destroyed five pillboxes, killing 20 Japanese soldiers and wiping out three machine guns that had been penning down American forces. His one-man assault inspired others and helped carry the day. Wounded by mortar fire, Lieutenant Terry died two days later. (NARA.)

In April 1946, Camp Robinson commander Col. Grover Graham presented the Bronze Star to Brig. Gen. S.L. Compere and his wife for their son Sgt. Powell Compere, who had been killed in action in France in January 1945 after almost three years of service. The war was over for those who sacrificed all and for those returning to civilian life in a free and grateful nation. Camp Robinson had served the nation proudly and the federal government returned it to the State of Arkansas to continue a mission of service. (NARA.)

Nine

THE MISSION NEVER ENDS

Camp Robinson today is home to the Arkansas National Guard, which continues the proud legacy of the hundreds of thousands of men and women who trained to serve the nation on the sprawling military post. The National Guard is the only branch of the nation's military operating with a dual mission. The guard is funded and trained to serve if called in wartime missions but equally ready to support civilian authorities when called in times of natural or manmade disasters. The National Guardsmen above are seen honing their skills with a mortar, exemplifying a nation of civilian soldiers ready if called to duty. (ANGM.)

The Camp Robinson Maneuver Training Center today consists of 35,000 acres boasting three of the National Guards' premier training centers: the 233rd Regiment Regional Training Institute; the National Guard Marksmanship Training Center, taking advantage of 26 small arms ranges; and the National Guard Professional Education Center. These exemplary schools draw 40,000 people annually from across the nation to hone their skills. In 2012, Camp Robinson supported almost 400,000 man-days of training. (ANGM.)

The Arkansas National Guard of today proudly claims a force of 10,000 soldiers and airmen within six major subordinate commands: the 39th Infantry Brigade Combat Team, 77th Theater Aviation Brigade, 87th Troop Command, 142nd Fires Brigade, 188th Fighter Wing, and the 189th Airlift Wing. These diverse expert commands link back to more than 60 different communities and armories across Arkansas, allowing for rapid deployment in times of need. (ANGM.)

Aside from the combat readiness work of modern-day Camp Robinson, the military post is also home to excellent military museums. Lloyd England Hall was built in 1932 as a multipurpose center at what was then Camp Pike; it became a post movie theater during World War II. Housing a museum since the 1970s, with major upgrades in the late 1990s, the museum, under the stewardship of retired colonel Steven Rucker, proudly showcases both the history of Camp Pike and Camp Robinson as well as the Arkansas National Guard. It is well worth a visit. (ANGM.)

In closing, this tribute to the military presence on the north shore of the Arkansas River is a solemn reminder that freedom is never free and that the Arkansas National Guard answers the call to battle still. Since September 11, 2001, a total of 20 members of the Arkansas National Guard have been killed in action on far-flung battlefields. They personify the best of what it means to be a citizen soldier, and they are owed a debt beyond measure. (ANGM.)

Discover Thousands of Local History Books Featuring Millions of Vintage Images

Arcadia Publishing, the leading local history publisher in the United States, is committed to making history accessible and meaningful through publishing books that celebrate and preserve the heritage of America's people and places.

Find more books like this at
www.arcadiapublishing.com

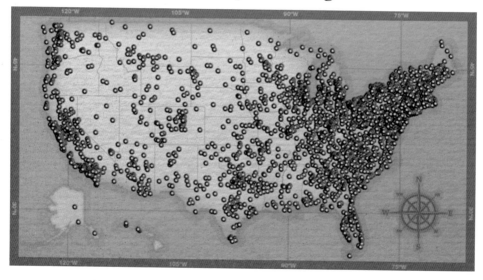

Search for your hometown history, your old stomping grounds, and even your favorite sports team.

Consistent with our mission to preserve history on a local level, this book was printed in South Carolina on American-made paper and manufactured entirely in the United States. Products carrying the accredited Forest Stewardship Council (FSC) label are printed on 100 percent FSC-certified paper.

MADE IN THE USA